101 HACKS FOR KIDS

BY ZOEY GRIFFIN

Copyright 2023 ©

All rights reserved.

No part of this book may be reproduced, distributed, or transmitted in any form or by any means, including photocopying, recording, or other electronic or mechanical methods, without the prior written permission of the publisher, except in the case of brief quotations in reviews and certain other non-commercial uses permitted by copyright law.

INTRODUCTION

In today's fast-paced and interconnected society, kids face a myriad of challenges, from academic pressures and social complexities to the influence of technology and media. As they strive to establish their independence, kids often encounter situations that require decision-making, problem-solving, and effective communication. This book aims to empower kids with a wide range of life skills that will serve as valuable assets throughout their lives. Throughout these pages, kids will discover engaging and age-appropriate guidance on a wide array of topics. They will explore the importance of self-care and well-being, learning to prioritize their mental and physical health. They will delve into the art of effective communication, discovering how to express themselves assertively and empathetically while actively listening to others. They will gain insights into managing their time and responsibilities, setting realistic goals, and developing a growth mindset that fosters a love for learning and personal development. Bridging the gap between childhood and adolescence, are a crucial period of self-discovery and growth. It is during this time that kids begin to forge their unique identities and develop the skills necessary to thrive in an ever-changing world!

GROWING UP WITH CONFIDENCE

For parents, guardians, and caregivers, guiding kids through this critical phase can sometimes feel like charting unfamiliar territory. The sheer magnitude of changes occurring in a kid's life can be overwhelming, leaving many adults uncertain about how best to support and nurture their young ones when growing up. This is precisely why this book was written – to equip you with the tools, knowledge, and strategies necessary to guide kids through these formative years with confidence.

Dear Kid:

Embrace your uniqueness. The kid years are a time when you're discovering who you are and what makes you special. Embrace your unique qualities and interests. Don't worry too much about fitting in or trying to be like everyone else. Celebrate what makes you different!

Take care of yourself. It's important to take care of both your physical and mental well-being. Eat nutritious food, get enough sleep, and stay active. Engage in activities that make you happy and help you relax. Remember to express your emotions and talk to someone you trust if you're feeling overwhelmed.

Set goals and work towards them. Setting goals can give you a sense of purpose and direction. Whether it's a school project, a hobby, or a personal challenge, break it down into smaller steps and work towards achieving them. Celebrate your progress along the way, and don't be discouraged by setbacks.

Communicate with your parents or guardians. Your parents or guardians are there to guide you and support you through this phase of life. Talk to them about your feelings, challenges, and successes. They can provide valuable advice and help you navigate any difficulties you may encounter.

Develop good habits. The kid years are a great time to develop healthy habits that can benefit you throughout your life. This includes things like good hygiene, staying organized, managing your time effectively, and being responsible with your commitments.

Explore your interests. Use this time to explore different activities and hobbies. Try new things, whether it's playing a musical instrument, joining a sports team, or joining a club at school. Discovering your passions and talents can boost your self-confidence and give you a sense of purpose.

EMPOWERING KIDS THROUGH THIS BOOK

This book is not just a mere guidebook but a companion that kids can turn to as they navigate the ups and downs of their childhood. It offers practical exercises, real-life examples, and thought-provoking reflections to encourage self-reflection and personal growth. With each skill explored, kids will gain the tools to face challenges with resilience, make informed decisions, and build a strong foundation for a fulfilling future.

Remember, kids, the journey you are embarking upon is filled with endless possibilities! As you develop these vital life skills, you will not only shape your own destiny but also contribute positively to your community and the world around you. So, dive in, explore, and let this book be your guiding light on this transformative journey. Good luck!

1. EFFECTIVE COMMUNICATION

Clear communication involves organizing thoughts, using appropriate language, and expressing ideas in a coherent manner. Use clear and simple language when communicating. You should express your thoughts and ideas in a way that others can easily understand.

Communication is not solely reliant on words. Non-verbal cues such as facial expressions, body language, and tone of voice play a crucial role in conveying messages. You should be aware of your nonverbal cues and learn to interpret those of others. Avoid interrupting or dismissing others' thoughts, even if you disagree.

It's important to express your emotions in a constructive and respectful manner. Use "I" statements to express your feelings, such as "I feel upset when..." instead of blaming or attacking others. This helps avoid misunderstandings and promotes open dialogue.

2. DIGITAL COMMUNICATION ETIQUETTE

Treat people online with the same respect and kindness as you would in person. Avoid using offensive language, making hurtful comments, or engaging in cyberbullying. Remember that there's a real person behind every username. Take a moment to consider the potential impact of your words or actions before posting or sharing anything online. Once something is out there, it can be challenging to undo.

Avoid using excessive slang, text speak, or abbreviations that may be difficult for others to understand. Communicate clearly and respectfully. Using proper grammar and spelling also demonstrates your maturity and professionalism. Online communication lacks the visual and auditory cues present in face-to-face conversations. Therefore, it's easy for messages to be misinterpreted. Be mindful of your tone and try to express yourself clearly. Use emojis or emoticons if necessary to convey the intended emotion.

Always ask for permission before sharing someone else's personal information or pictures. Avoid sharing your own personal information, such as your home address or phone number, in public forums or with people you don't know well. Respect others' online boundaries and be considerate of their time and preferences. If someone doesn't respond or seems uninterested, don't push them for a response.

3. ACTIVE LISTENING

Focus your attention on the speaker and maintain eye contact. Put away distractions like electronic devices and show that you value their words. Display your interest through verbal and non-verbal cues. Nodding, smiling, and asking relevant questions demonstrate that you are engaged in the conversation.

Let the speaker finish their thoughts before responding. Interrupting can disrupt the flow of conversation and make the speaker feel unheard. After the speaker has finished talking, summarize what you understood from their message. This shows that you were actively listening and helps clarify any misunderstandings. Try to understand the speaker's emotions and perspective. Show empathy by acknowledging their feelings and offering support or encouragement when appropriate.

Sometimes conversations can be challenging or lengthy. Practice patience and avoid rushing the speaker. Remember, active listening requires time and effort!

4. PUBLIC SPEAKING

Public speaking helps you become a better communicator. It allows you to express your thoughts and ideas clearly, persuasively, and confidently. This skill will be useful not only in school presentations but also in everyday conversations, job interviews, and future career opportunities. Here are a few simple steps:

1. Begin by speaking in front of small groups of friends, family, or classmates. This will help you gain confidence and experience without feeling overwhelmed.

2. Take time to prepare your speech or presentation. Practice your speech multiple times to familiarize yourself with the content and improve your delivery.

3. Pay attention to your body language while speaking. Stand tall, maintain good posture, and make eye contact with the audience.

4. Pace yourself and speak slowly and clearly. This will make it easier for your audience to understand you.

5. Incorporate visual aids such as slides, props, or charts to enhance your presentation.

6. It's normal to feel nervous before speaking in public. Practice deep breathing exercises or visualization techniques to calm your nerves. Remember that everyone makes mistakes, and even experienced speakers get nervous at times.

7. Consider joining a public speaking club or taking a public speaking class.

5. READING AND INTERPRETING NONVERBAL CUES

- Pay attention to people's body language, such as facial expressions, gestures, and posture. These can provide valuable clues about their thoughts and emotions. Notice if someone is smiling, frowning, crossing their arms, or making eye contact, as these nonverbal cues can reveal a lot about their feelings.

- Nonverbal cues should be interpreted in the context of the situation. So, consider the environment, the relationship between the people involved, and the overall situation to get a better understanding of the nonverbal cues being displayed. For example, a person might yawn because they are tired, not necessarily because they are bored.

- Using a mirror can help you become more aware of your body language and how it may be interpreted by others. By recognizing your own nonverbal cues, you can develop better control over your communication and be more sensitive to others' nonverbal cues.

- Ask for feedback from trusted individuals, such as parents, teachers, or friends, regarding their interpretation of nonverbal cues. This feedback can help you refine your understanding and improve your skills in reading and interpreting nonverbal cues.

- Remember, the combination of verbal and nonverbal cues provides a more complete understanding of the message being conveyed!

6. CONFLICT RESOLUTION

- When faced with a conflict, try to stay calm and composed. Take a deep breath and avoid letting your emotions take over. Remaining calm will help you think clearly and find a better solution.

- One of the most important aspects of conflict resolution is active listening. Pay attention to what the other person is saying without interrupting or judging. Show that you are genuinely interested in understanding their perspective.

- Clearly communicate your thoughts and feelings using "I" statements. For example, say "I feel hurt when..." instead of blaming or accusing the other person. Being assertive allows you to express yourself effectively without becoming aggressive or passive.

o If you realize that you have made a mistake or hurt someone, be willing to apologize sincerely.

o Look for common ground and try to find a solution that benefits both parties. Compromise means both sides give a little and find a middle ground. Remember, it's not about winning or losing but finding a resolution that satisfies everyone involved. Work collaboratively to find solutions.

o Every conflict can be a learning opportunity. By learning from conflicts, you can grow and develop better strategies for resolving conflicts in the future.

7. NEGOTIATION SKILLS

o Before entering into a negotiation, do your homework. Understand the subject matter, gather relevant information, and anticipate the other person's perspective. This knowledge will boost your confidence and help you make persuasive arguments.

o Identify what you want to achieve from the negotiation. Set specific and realistic goals, and prioritize them.

o Listening attentively is crucial in negotiations. Pay attention to the other person's viewpoint and ask questions to clarify their position.

- Use clear and concise language to express your thoughts. Be respectful and maintain a positive tone throughout the negotiation.

- Approach negotiation as a problem-solving exercise rather than a competition. Seek creative solutions that address the interests of both parties.

- Believe in yourself and your abilities. Confidence is key when negotiating, as it influences how others perceive your arguments.

- Negotiation skills improve with practice. Look for opportunities to negotiate in different settings, such as school projects or group activities.

8. SELF-AWARENESS

Spend some time each day reflecting on your thoughts, feelings, and actions. This can be done through journaling or simply sitting quietly and thinking about your experiences. Try to recognize the different emotions you experience and label them accordingly.

Practice mindfulness techniques such as deep breathing, meditation, or body scans. These practices can help you become more present in the moment and increase your self-awareness by noticing your thoughts, sensations, and emotions without judgment.

Seek feedback from trusted adults, such as parents, teachers, or mentors. Constructive feedback can provide valuable insights into your strengths and areas for improvement, helping you develop a clearer understanding of yourself. Try different activities and explore various interests. By engaging in different hobbies, sports, or artistic pursuits, you can discover what you truly enjoy and what resonates with you. This exploration will foster self-awareness by highlighting your preferences and talents.

9. SELF-ACCEPTANCE

Embrace your uniqueness! Recognize and celebrate the qualities that make you different from others. Whether it's your appearance, talents, or personality traits, understand that diversity is what makes the world interesting. It's easy to compare yourself to others, especially with the influence of social media. Remember that people usually present a filtered and curated version of their lives. Instead, focus on your growth and progress rather than comparing yourself to others. Pay attention to your inner voice and how it speaks to you. Replace self-critical thoughts with positive and affirming statements, practicing self-compassion.

If you're struggling with self-acceptance or experiencing negative emotions, don't hesitate to reach out for support. Talk to a trusted adult, such as a parent, teacher, or counselor, who can provide guidance and help you navigate through challenges. Learn to embrace your strengths and accept your weaknesses. Self-awareness includes recognizing and acknowledging both positive and negative aspects of oneself. Remember – nobody is perfect, and it's important to love and accept yourself unconditionally.

10. CULTIVATE AN ATTITUDE OF GRATITUDE

- Start a gratitude journal. Set aside a few minutes each day to write down three things you are grateful for. It could be as simple as a sunny day, a delicious meal, or spending time with friends. Writing them down helps you focus on the positive aspects of your life.

- Make it a habit to express gratitude to the people around you! Thank your parents, siblings, teachers, and friends for the things they do for you. Compliment and acknowledge their efforts, kindness, and support.

- Volunteer and help others. By making a positive difference in someone else's life, you'll cultivate gratitude and a sense of purpose.

- When faced with challenges or setbacks, try to find the positive aspects or lessons within them. This can help you develop resilience and gratitude for the growth opportunities that come from adversity.

- Encourage your family members to share what they are grateful for during meals or designated family time. This fosters a supportive environment and allows everyone to appreciate the blessings in their lives.

11. BASIC COOKING SKILLS

○ Begin by choosing recipes that have fewer ingredients and simpler steps. This allows you to focus on mastering basic techniques without feeling overwhelmed.

○ Read through the entire recipe before starting and gather all the required ingredients and equipment. Follow the instructions step by step, paying attention to measurements and cooking times.

○ Learn about kitchen safety, including proper hand washing, handling hot objects, using oven mitts, and being cautious around stovetops and other appliances. Always have adult supervision when dealing with heat or potentially dangerous tasks.

○ Always be cautious and have adult supervision when using sharp objects like a knife.

- Familiarize yourself with basic cooking techniques like boiling, sautéing, baking, and grilling. Each method requires different heat levels and cooking times, so understanding these techniques will broaden your culinary skills.

- Clean up as you go! Make it a habit to clean as you cook. It will help keep your workspace organized and make cleanup easier when you're done.

- Don't hesitate to ask for help or guidance from a parent, guardian, or experienced adult when needed. They can provide valuable tips and ensure your safety in the kitchen. Practice and have fun!

12. TIME MANAGEMENT

Start by identifying the most important tasks or activities that need your attention. Make a to-do list and prioritize them based on their importance and urgency. This way, you can focus on what truly matters and avoid wasting time on less essential things.

Use a planner, calendar, or digital tools to create a schedule that outlines your daily activities, including homework, extracurricular activities, chores, and leisure time. A schedule helps you allocate time for each task and ensures that you have enough time for everything without feeling overwhelmed. Sometimes tasks may seem overwhelming, and you might feel unsure of where to start. Break larger tasks into smaller, manageable steps. This way, you can approach them one at a time, making them more achievable and less stressful. Reward yourself after completing each step. This way, you'll stay motivated and avoid unnecessary stress. Identify common distractions like social media, video games, or TV, and set boundaries for yourself. Designate specific times for using these activities as rewards for completing tasks rather than letting them consume your time excessively!

13. TIME BLOCKING

Divide your day into time blocks, assigning specific durations for each activity or task. For example, you could have a block for schoolwork, another for physical activity or hobbies, and another for relaxation or free time. Make sure to consider your energy levels and concentration span when assigning time blocks.

Use a planner or calendar to create a visual representation of your time blocks. Write down the activities or tasks you will focus on during each block. Be realistic and allocate sufficient time for each task. Remember to include breaks and transition time between activities. Once you've created your time-blocking schedule, make a commitment to follow it as closely as possible. Treat each time block as a dedicated period for that specific activity. Avoid distractions and try to stay focused on the task at hand during each block. At the end of each day or week, review how well you adhered to your time-blocking schedule!

14. GOAL SETTING

- Start by thinking about what you want to achieve. It could be something related to school, hobbies, sports, personal development, or anything else that interests you. Be specific about what you want to accomplish.

- Goals need a timeframe to work towards. Determine when you want to achieve your goal. Breaking down big goals into smaller milestones can help you track progress.

- It's important to set goals that are achievable. While it's great to dream big, it's also essential to consider your abilities and available resources.

- Outline the specific actions you need to take to reach your goal. Write down your plan or use a goal-setting worksheet to make it clear and organized.

- Goal setting requires dedication and perseverance. It's important to stay focused and motivated, especially when faced with challenges or setbacks.

- Regularly review your progress and make any necessary adjustments. Sometimes, circumstances change, or you might discover new information that affects your goal. It's okay to modify your plan if needed, as long as it helps you stay on track and move forward.

15. DECISION MAKING

- First, you need to know what decision you need to make.

- Once you know what the decision is about, try to gather as much information as possible. This can include researching, asking questions, and talking to people who have experience or knowledge about the topic.

- Think about the different choices or possibilities available to you. It's helpful to write them down or make a list. Sometimes it's also useful to consider the pros and cons of each option.

- Once you have a list of options, think about each one and evaluate how well it aligns with your goals, values, and priorities. Consider the potential outcomes or consequences of each option.

- Based on the information and evaluation, make a decision. Trust your instincts and what feels right to you. Remember, it's normal to feel a bit uncertain or worried sometimes, but try to have confidence in your choice.

- After making a decision, it's time to take action and put your choice into practice. Think about what worked well and what didn't. This can help you learn from your decisions and improve your future decision-making skills.

16. PROBLEM-SOLVING SKILLS

- The first step is to clearly understand and define the problem you're facing. Take some time to think about what the issue is and what you're trying to achieve.

- Once you've defined the problem, gather all the relevant information about it. This might involve asking questions, doing research, or talking to others who have faced similar problems.

- Next, brainstorm a list of possible solutions. Encourage yourself to think creatively and come up with as many ideas as you can, without worrying about whether they're feasible or not. This step is all about exploring different options.

- After generating a list of potential solutions, evaluate each one based on its pros and cons. Consider the advantages and disadvantages of each solution, as well as any potential risks or consequences. Based on your evaluation, select the solution that seems most effective and practical. Remember that there might not always be a perfect solution, but aim for the one that addresses the problem in the best way possible.

- Once you've chosen a solution, create a step-by-step action plan to implement it. Put your plan into action and start working on solving the problem. Be prepared to adapt and make adjustments if necessary. Good luck!

17. CRITICAL THINKING

Critical thinking starts with asking questions. Instead of accepting information at face value, you learn to question and explore it further. You might ask yourself, "Why is this true?" or "How do I know if this information is reliable?"

Once you have a question in mind, critical thinking involves breaking down the information or situation into smaller parts to understand it better. It's like solving a puzzle piece by piece. Next, you need to evaluate the information or situation. This means examining its strengths and weaknesses, considering different perspectives, and thinking about the consequences or potential outcomes. You might ask yourself, "Is this a good idea?" or "What are the pros and cons?"

Critical thinking also involves reasoning. It's about using logical thinking to draw conclusions or make decisions based on the information you have gathered. Critical thinkers are open to new ideas and willing to consider different viewpoints. They listen to others, respect different opinions, and are willing to change their own views if they find better evidence or reasoning.

18. HOW TO DEVELOP EMPATHY

Empathy is an important quality that helps us understand and share the feelings of other people. It means putting yourself in someone else's shoes and trying to imagine how they might be feeling.

Imagine you see one of your friends feeling sad or upset about something. If you have empathy, you can recognize that your friend is feeling down, and you can try to understand why they might be feeling that way. Maybe they had a bad day at school, or maybe something happened at home that made them upset. Instead of ignoring their feelings or making them feel worse, empathy allows you to offer support and show kindness.

Empathy is not just about understanding someone's emotions; it also involves taking action. It's about showing compassion and doing something to help others feel better. For example, if you notice your friend is sad, you can lend a listening ear and let them talk about what's bothering them. You can offer words of encouragement or even a simple gesture like a hug or a smile to let them know you care.

19. HOW TO BUILD YOUR RESILIENCE

Resilience starts with having confidence in yourself. Remember that you are capable of handling whatever comes your way. Believe in your abilities and strengths, and know that you have the power to overcome challenges.

When faced with tough situations, it's important to maintain a positive attitude. Try to focus on the good things and look for silver linings even in difficult times. Remember, a positive mindset can help you find solutions and see the brighter side of things. It's normal to feel sad, angry, or frustrated when things don't go as planned. Allow yourself to experience these emotions and understand that it's okay to feel them. Talk to someone you trust, like a parent or a friend, about how you're feeling. Expressing your emotions can help you process them and find support. Everyone makes mistakes, and that's how we learn and grow. When you face setbacks or make errors, try to see them as opportunities for growth. Think about what you can learn from the experience and how you can do things differently next time!

20. HOW TO HAVE PATIENCE IN LIFE

Sometimes we have to wait for things we want, like a turn on the swing or waiting for a special day. Remember that waiting is a normal part of life, and it teaches us important lessons. Instead of always thinking about what will happen next, try to focus on what you're doing right now. Enjoy the present moment and make the most of it. This will help time feel like it's passing more quickly. Instead of just sitting and waiting, find something fun or interesting to do. You can read a book, play a game, draw, or talk to a friend. This way, waiting won't feel as boring, and time will go by faster. Waiting can teach us essential lessons, like being patient, understanding others, or being more appreciative. Pay attention to what you learn during the waiting process and try to grow as a person.

If you're finding it difficult to be patient, don't hesitate to ask for help. Talk to your parents, teachers, or friends about how you're feeling.

21. HOW TO BE ASSERTIVE

Understand that you have the right to express yourself and your opinions. Your thoughts and feelings matter, and it's important to remember that you deserve to be heard. Your body language can say a lot about how confident you feel. Stand tall, make eye contact, and use hand gestures to emphasize your points. This shows that you are confident in what you're saying.

Assertiveness is not just about expressing yourself; it also involves listening to others. When someone else is speaking, pay attention, maintain eye contact, and show interest in what they're saying. This demonstrates respect and helps build better communication. Learn to say "no": It's okay to say "no" when you feel uncomfortable or when you don't want to do something. Practice saying it in a polite but firm way. Remember, you don't have to please everyone all the time, and it's important to respect your own boundaries. Find a friend or family member and practice different scenarios where you need to be assertive. This can help you build confidence and find the right words to express yourself effectively.

22. COLLABORATION AND TEAMWORK

Collaboration and teamwork are focused on a shared objective. It could be completing a school project, organizing a class event, or even playing a team sport. Everyone involved in the collaboration works towards achieving that goal. It's like everyone is on the same team, supporting each other to succeed.

Each person in a team brings their unique strengths, talents, and skills to the table. Some might be good at organizing things, while others are great at coming up with creative ideas. By combining these strengths, the team becomes more powerful and can solve problems more effectively. Collaboration and teamwork rely on good communication. It means expressing your thoughts clearly and listening to others. By working with different people, we expand our knowledge and grow as individuals. When we work together, we can enjoy the process and build friendships. It's exciting to see how everyone's contributions come together and create something amazing!

23. HOW TO DEVELOP LEADERSHIP SKILLS

- Good leaders listen attentively to others. Practice active listening by paying attention when someone is speaking to you. Show interest, maintain eye contact, and ask questions to understand their thoughts and feelings.

- Set a positive example for others to follow. Be respectful, kind, and responsible in your words and actions. When you demonstrate good behavior, others will be inspired to do the same.

- Look for opportunities to help others or improve your surroundings. Offer assistance, organize activities, or suggest solutions to problems. Taking initiative shows responsibility and inspires others to follow your lead.

- Leaders understand the power of teamwork. Collaborate with your peers on projects or activities. Learn to appreciate and value everyone's contributions!

- Leaders have a vision and set goals to achieve it. Identify what you want to accomplish and create a plan to reach your objectives.

- Great leaders understand and care about the needs of others. Practice empathy by putting yourself in someone else's shoes and understanding their feelings and perspectives.

- Read books, explore new subjects, and seek out opportunities to develop your skills. Attend workshops, join clubs or organizations, and surround yourself with positive role models who can guide and inspire you.

24. LEARN ORGANIZATION SKILLS

- It's easier to stay organized when your surroundings are tidy. Begin by cleaning up your room or study area. Put away toys, books, and other items in their proper places.

- Get yourself a planner or use a calendar to keep track of important dates, such as assignments, tests, and activities. Write down your schedule and check it regularly so you don't forget anything.

- Assign specific places for your belongings, like a shelf for books or a box for toys. When you're done using something, put it back in its designated spot. This will help you find things easily and avoid clutter. Labels and folders can be helpful for keeping things organized.

- Set aside some time each day or week to tidy up your space. This could involve putting away toys, sorting out your backpack, or organizing your study materials. Regular clean-ups will prevent messes from piling up.

- Establishing a daily routine can be very helpful. Set specific times for activities like homework, playtime, and chores. If you're feeling overwhelmed or unsure about how to get organized, don't hesitate to ask for help. Talk to your parents, teachers, or older siblings.

25. BASIC FINANCIAL LITERACY

Money is what we use to buy things. It's important to know that money has value and that we need to earn it by doing work or getting an allowance.

Saving means putting money aside for future use. It's a good habit to save a portion of the money you earn or receive as a gift. You can use a piggy bank or a savings account at a bank to keep your savings safe.

Earning money teaches you the value of hard work and helps you become responsible with your finances. You can earn money by doing chores, helping others, or starting a small business like a lemonade stand or pet sitting.

Spending wisely – when you spend your money, it's important to make smart choices. Think about whether you need something before buying it. Compare prices, read reviews, and consider if it's worth the money.

Giving and sharing – it's important to learn about giving and sharing. You can donate a portion of your money or time to help others in need. This teaches empathy, gratitude, and the importance of contributing to your community.

Investments are ways to make your money grow over time. As you get older, you can explore concepts like stocks, bonds, and mutual funds. It's important to learn about investing and seek advice from trusted adults before making any investment decisions.

26. BUDGETING AND MANAGING MONEY

Think about the things you want to save money for. It could be a new toy, a special trip, or even saving for the future. Having goals will help you stay motivated and focused. Keep track of the money you receive, whether it's from allowances, gifts, or doing chores. Write it down or use a money-tracking app if you have one. This will help you see how much money you have and how you're spending it.

Understand the difference between needs and wants. Needs are things like food, clothes, and school supplies that are necessary for everyday life. Wants are things like toys, games, or treats that you may like to have but can live without. It's important to prioritize needs over wants when you're budgeting. Start by listing your income (the money you receive) and then think about your expenses (the things you need to spend money on). Once you have a budget, plan how you'll spend your money. Think about what's most important to you and allocate your money accordingly. It's a good idea to save some money for unexpected expenses too.

27. HOW TO CLEAN YOUR HOME

Creating a cleaning schedule helps you plan which chores to do and when to do them. You can divide chores into daily, weekly, and monthly tasks.

Before you start cleaning, gather all the supplies you'll need. This may include a broom, mop, vacuum cleaner, dustpan, duster, cleaning sprays, sponges, and gloves. Having everything ready will make your cleaning tasks easier. Before you start cleaning, it's a good idea to declutter and organize your belongings. Pick up toys, put away clothes, and organize books and school supplies. Having a tidy space will make it easier to clean. Use a duster or a damp cloth to dust surfaces like tables, shelves, and countertops. Wipe away any dust or dirt to keep your surfaces clean and shiny. Then, use a vacuum cleaner to clean carpets, rugs, and floors. Pay attention to corners and under furniture where dust can accumulate. For hard floors, like tile or wood, use a mop or a damp cloth to wipe away any dirt or spills.

Assist with mealtime clean-up. After meals, help clear the table, wash dishes, or load the dishwasher. Wipe down the countertops and sweep the floor to keep the kitchen clean and tidy.

28. BASIC SEWING

Gather your supplies – you'll need a needle, thread, scissors, and the item you want to sew or mend. Cut a piece of thread about twice the length of your arm. Insert one end of the thread through the eye of the needle and pull it through until you have two equal-length threads. Tie a knot at the end. There are two basic stitches you'll need to know: the running stitch and the backstitch. Running stitch is the simplest stitch. Push the needle up through the fabric from the back and then back down, creating a straight line of stitches. Repeat this process until you reach the end of the area you want to sew. Backstitch is stronger than the running stitch and is used for mending seams. Push the needle up through the fabric from the back and then back down a short distance ahead. Then, bring the needle up just behind the last stitch and push it back down through the same hole. Repeat this process until you reach the end of the area you want to sew.

Place the fabric you want to sew on a flat surface. Hold the two pieces together firmly with your non-dominant hand. With your dominant hand, push the needle through the fabric, following the line you want to sew. Pull the thread through until the knot stops it. Continue sewing using either the running stitch or backstitch, depending on the project.

29. HOW TO SEW A BUTTON

Thread your needle – Take your thread and cut a piece that's about one and a half times the length of your arm. Then, take one end of the thread and pass it through the eye of the needle. Pull the thread through until both ends are even and tie a knot at the end.

Position the button – Decide where you want to sew your button. Place it on the fabric and make a small mark with a pen or a pencil where you want the center of the button to be.

Anchor the thread – Insert the needle from the backside of the fabric, coming up through one of the holes in the button. Pull the thread until the knot at the end catches on the fabric, securing the thread in place. You can also make an extra knot on the backside for added security.

Sew the button – Now, it's time to sew the button in place. Insert the needle down through another hole diagonally opposite to the first hole. Pull the thread until the button sits snugly on the fabric.

Create stitches – Insert the needle back up through one of the remaining holes. Then, insert it down through the hole diagonally opposite. Repeat this process, creating a crisscross pattern of stitches on the backside of the fabric.

Secure the thread – After making several crisscross stitches, bring the needle to the backside of the fabric. Pass it through a few stitches or make a small loop under the button. This will secure the thread in place. Trim any excess thread with a pair of scissors.

30. LAUNDRY SKILLS

Start by sorting your laundry into different piles. You can have separate piles for clothes, towels, and sheets. This helps to keep different types of fabrics and colors separate, so they don't get damaged or bleed onto each other. Before you start washing, make sure to check the care labels on your clothes. They provide important information about how to wash and dry them.

Once your laundry is sorted, it's time to load the washing machine. Open the machine and put your clothes in, being careful not to overload it. Next, add the right amount of laundry detergent. Follow the instructions on the detergent bottle to determine the correct amount. Close the machine and choose the appropriate cycle and water temperature for your clothes. After the washing cycle is complete, it's time to dry your clothes. If you have a dryer, place the clothes inside and set the appropriate temperature and drying time. If you don't have a dryer, you can hang your clothes on a clothesline or drying rack. Once your clothes are dry, it's time to fold them neatly. You can also use hangers for clothes that need to be hung, like dresses or jackets.

31. OTHER HOUSEHOLD CHORES

1. Washing dishes is an important chore after meals. You can help by rinsing dishes, loading them into the dishwasher, or washing them by hand with soap and water. You can also help with drying and putting away the clean dishes.

2. Then, you can set the table by placing plates, utensils, napkins, and glasses in their proper places. It's a fun way to contribute to the family and get ready for a meal together!

3. You can assist in collecting and tying up garbage bags and taking them outside to the trash cans.

4. You can make your own bed in the morning or assist in making your family members' beds. This involves straightening the sheets, fluffing pillows, and arranging the blankets.

5. If you have plants at home, you can help with watering them. Use a small watering can or a cup to carefully pour water onto the plants.

32. HOW TO ESTIMATE TIME ACCURATELY

- Time estimation is all about guessing or figuring out how long something will take. It's like making a prediction about how much time you think an activity or task will require.

- Imagine you want to make a delicious cake. Before you start, you might try to estimate how much time it will take to make the cake. You could look at the recipe and think about the steps involved. You might say, "Hmm, I think it will take me about 1 hour to mix the ingredients and bake the cake." That's your time estimation!

- Time estimation is helpful because it allows us to plan and manage our activities better. If you have a lot of things to do in a day, estimating how long each task will take can help you decide what to do first and how to schedule your time. It's like having a little clock in your head that helps you make decisions. But remember, time estimation is not always perfect! Sometimes things take longer than we think, and other times they might be quicker. That's okay! It's all part of learning and improving our time estimation skills.

33. HOW TO SET BOUNDARIES

Think about what makes you feel good and what makes you uncomfortable or upset. Boundaries can be about physical things, like personal space or possessions, or they can be about how others talk to you or treat you. For example, you might not want someone to touch your things without asking, or you may not like it when someone makes fun of you. Once you know your boundaries, it's important to let others know about them. For example, you can say, "I don't like it when you take my toys without asking. Please ask me first."

Sometimes, people may try to push your boundaries or not take them seriously. In those situations, it's important to be firm and stand up for yourself. Stay confident and don't let others make you feel bad for setting boundaries. If someone asks you to do something that you don't want to do or makes you uncomfortable, it's okay to say "no" politely but firmly. If someone continues to ignore or disrespect your boundaries, it's essential to seek help from a trusted adult, like a parent, teacher, or counselor.

34. HOW TO PRACTICE MINDFULNESS

1. Start by finding a quiet space where you can sit comfortably. It can be your bedroom, a quiet corner, or anywhere else where you feel relaxed.

2. Close your eyes or keep them softly focused. Take a few deep breaths and notice the sensation of your breath going in and out. Feel your belly rise and fall with each breath.

3. As you sit quietly, thoughts and feelings may come into your mind. That's okay! Just observe them without judgment. Imagine them as clouds passing by in the sky.

4. Take a few moments to scan your body from head to toe. Notice any sensations, tension, or areas of relaxation. If you find any areas of tension, imagine your breath flowing into those areas and helping them relax.

5. Bring your attention to your senses. What can you hear, see, smell, taste, or touch? Pay attention to the details of your surroundings, noticing the colors, sounds, and textures.

6. Take a moment to think about something or someone you feel grateful for. Allow yourself to feel the warmth and happiness that gratitude brings.

7. Remember that you can always come back to this present moment whenever you need to feel calm and centered.

35. INTERNET SAFETY GUIDE

- Never share your full name, address, phone number, or other personal information online without your parents' permission. This includes avoiding sharing personal information in public chats or on social media. People you don't know might try to use that information inappropriately or harmfully.

- It's fun to share photos and videos with friends and family, but be cautious about what you share. Avoid sharing pictures or videos that reveal too much about your location, daily routines, or personal activities.

- Just like in the real world, you should be cautious when interacting with strangers online. Be careful when talking to someone you don't know in person, and never agree to meet someone you've only met online without your parents' permission.

- Be careful when clicking on links or opening attachments in emails, messages, or on websites. Some links or files can contain viruses or harmful content that can damage your computer or steal your personal information.

- When creating passwords for your online accounts, use a combination of letters, numbers, and symbols.

Avoid using easily guessable information like your name or birthdate. It's also important to use different passwords for different accounts so that if one gets compromised, the others remain safe.

- Be mindful of cyberbullying. Cyberbullying is when someone uses the internet or digital devices to harass, intimidate, or hurt others. If you experience cyberbullying, don't respond to the messages or comments, and tell a trusted adult about it.

- Always communicate with your parents or guardians about your online activities. Let them know which websites you visit, who you're talking to, and if anything makes you uncomfortable. They are there to guide and protect you.

36. HOW TO RESEARCH A TOPIC

Write down everything you already know about the topic. This will help you figure out what you need to find out. Think of questions you have about the topic. For example, if you're researching dolphins, you might ask, "What do dolphins eat?" or "Where do dolphins live?" Write down all your questions. Go to the library or look for books at home about your topic. Ask a grown-up for help and use a safe search engine or trusted websites to find information online. Type in your questions or keywords related to your topic. As you find answers to your questions, write them down. Write down important facts and where you found them, like the book title or website address. If you still have questions, ask someone who knows a lot about the topic. It could be a teacher, a librarian, or maybe even a scientist or a specialist. They can give you more information and help you understand the topic better.

Once you have gathered all the information, organize it in a way that makes sense to you. You can make a mind map, create a list, or use headings and subheadings to categorize your notes.

37. SELF-DEFENSE TECHNIQUES

- The first and most important self-defense technique is being aware of your surroundings. Pay attention to what's happening around you and trust your instincts. If something doesn't feel right, it's best to stay away or seek help.

- If someone makes you feel uncomfortable or tries to approach you, it's okay to use your voice. Loudly and confidently say "No!" or "Stop!" to let them know you're not okay with their behavior. This can attract attention and discourage them from continuing.

- Running is often the best option in dangerous situations. If you feel threatened, quickly get away from the person or situation. Run towards a safe place where there are other people around.

- If you can't escape and you need to defend yourself physically, aim for the person's vulnerable areas. These include the eyes, nose, throat, groin, and knees. Use your hands, elbows, or legs to strike these areas and create an opportunity to escape.

- Learn basic blocking techniques to protect yourself if someone tries to grab you. For example, if someone grabs your wrist, twist your arm to free yourself, or pull your hand towards your body and twist it out of their grip. Once you're free, run away as quickly as possible!

38. BASIC FIRST AID

- The first thing to do in any emergency situation is to stay calm. If you come across someone who is seriously injured or very sick, the first thing you should do is call for help. This means finding an adult or calling emergency services like 911, depending on where you live.

- Before you try to help someone, it's important to make sure the area is safe for both of you. Look around for any potential dangers, such as fire, traffic, or falling objects.

- ABC – Airway, Breathing, Circulation. These are three important things to check in an injured person. First, check if their airway is clear by looking inside their mouth and removing any visible objects or obstructions. Then, check if they are breathing by watching their chest for movement. Finally, check for a pulse to see if their heart is beating.

- If someone is bleeding, you can help by applying direct pressure to the wound with a clean cloth or your hand.

- Sometimes, the most important thing you can do is to provide comfort and support to the person who is injured or sick!

39. HOW TO PERFORM CPR

- Before you start, make sure the area is safe. Look around for any dangers or hazards that could harm you or the person you're helping.

- Place one of your hands, the one you write with, on the center of the person's chest (between the nipples). Put your other hand on top, and interlock your fingers. Keep your arms straight and position yourself directly over the person's chest. Press down hard and fast, about two inches deep, at a rate of 100-120 compressions per minute. Try to do 30 compressions in a row.

- Tilt the person's head back again and lift their chin to open the airway. Pinch their nose closed with your thumb and index finger. Take a normal breath, seal your mouth over theirs, and blow gently until you see their chest rise. Give two rescue breaths, each lasting about one second.

○ Repeat chest compressions and rescue breaths: Continue with 30 chest compressions followed by two rescue breaths. Keep doing this until help arrives, or the person starts breathing on their own, or you're too tired to continue. Remember to call for help again if there's no one doing it already.

40. BASIC ETIQUETTE AND MANNERS

○ Saying "Please" and "Thank you": Using these words shows gratitude and appreciation. When you ask for something, say "Please," and when someone does something nice for you, say "Thank you."

○ When you meet someone or enter a room, it's polite to say "Hello" or "Hi." It shows that you acknowledge the other person's presence.

○ Using words like "Excuse me," "I'm sorry," and "May I" are important. If you accidentally bump into someone, say "I'm sorry." If you need to get someone's attention, say "Excuse me." And if you want something, ask, "May I please have...?"

○ Sharing your toys, games, or snacks is a kind gesture. It helps others feel included and shows that you care about their happiness.

- When eating with others, use your utensils (fork, spoon, and knife) properly. Chew with your mouth closed, don't talk with food in your mouth, and ask to be excused before leaving the table.
- Treat others the way you would like to be treated.

41. MAP READING AND NAVIGATION

Maps are drawings or pictures that show us what a place looks like from above. They can be of a city, a country, or even the whole world! Maps have many different symbols and colors that represent different things, like roads, buildings, rivers, and mountains. To read a map, you need to understand these symbols and colors. For example, a blue line might represent a river, while a brown line could be a road. By looking at the symbols and colors, you can figure out where things are located on the map.

Navigation is the process of figuring out where you are on a map and how to get to a specific place. It's like following a treasure map! To navigate, you need to know some important things. The first thing is the compass rose, which shows you which way is north, south, east, and west on the map. North is usually at the top of the map. You can also use landmarks, which are easily recognizable features on the map, like a big mountain or a tall building.

42. STUDY SKILLS

1. It's important to keep your study materials and workspace organized. Have a designated place for your books, notebooks, and supplies. Keep your study area tidy so that you can focus better and find what you need easily.

2. Make a study schedule that includes specific times for studying and breaks. Having a routine will help you develop a habit of studying regularly. Remember to include breaks in your schedule to rest and recharge your brain.

3. When you're listening to a teacher or reading a textbook, take notes to help you remember important information. Use keywords and short phrases instead of writing everything word-for-word. Review your notes later to reinforce what you've learned.

4. When you're reading a book or a passage, try to actively engage with the material. Ask yourself questions about what you're reading and make connections to what you already know.

5. Regular practice is essential for learning and retaining information. After you've learned something new, review it periodically to reinforce your memory. Practice problems, quizzes, and flashcards can be helpful tools to test your knowledge and understanding.

6. Don't be afraid to ask for help if you're having trouble understanding something. Talk to your teacher, parents, or classmates if you need clarification or additional guidance.

43. HOW TO LEARN A NEW LANGUAGE

- Decide what you want to achieve with your language learning. It could be learning some basic phrases, having conversations, or even becoming fluent. Setting goals will help you stay motivated!

- Look for resources that will help you learn the language. You can find books, websites, apps, and even language-learning videos online.

- Begin by learning the basics, like greetings, numbers, colors, and simple phrases. Practice saying them out loud to get comfortable with the sounds of the language.

- Flashcards are a great tool to help you remember new words and phrases. Write the word or phrase in the language you're learning on one side of the card and the translation on the other side. Test yourself by flipping the cards and trying to remember the translation.

- Listening to native speakers is an excellent way to improve your pronunciation and understanding of the language. Watch movies, listen to songs, or find podcasts in the language you're learning. Try to practice a little bit every day.

- Learning a new language can be challenging at times, but remember to have fun with it! Explore the culture associated with the language, try cooking a traditional dish, or learn some fun songs or rhymes.

44. ACTIVE PARTICIPATION IN SCHOOL

Start by coming to school ready to learn. Make sure you have all your necessary school supplies, such as books, notebooks, and pencils. Completing your homework and assignments on time will also help you stay prepared. When your teacher is explaining something or giving instructions, listen attentively. Ask questions if you don't understand something or need clarification. Participate in class discussions by sharing your thoughts and ideas. It's important to be an active listener and engage in the learning process.

Taking notes during class is a great way to stay engaged and remember important information. Write down key points, definitions, and examples shared by the teacher. Complete your assignments and homework to the best of your ability. This shows your dedication to learning and helps you practice what you've learned in class. If you need help, don't hesitate to ask your teacher or a classmate for assistance.

Participating in extracurricular activities, such as sports teams, clubs, or music groups, allows you to explore your interests and develop new skills. It's a chance to engage with other students who share similar hobbies or passions. Look for opportunities to help your classmates or contribute to the school community.

45. VOLUNTEER WORK

Volunteer work is when people give their time and skills to help others or make a positive difference in their communities, without expecting to get paid. It's a way to show kindness, and compassion, and make the world a better place. There are many different types of volunteer work that kids can get involved in. For example, you can volunteer at a local animal shelter and help take care of the animals by feeding them, cleaning their cages, or even playing with them. This helps ensure that the animals are happy and healthy while they wait to find their forever homes.

Another way to volunteer is by participating in environmental projects. You can join a beach cleanup to pick up trash and protect marine life, or help plant trees and create green spaces in your neighborhood. These activities help take care of our planet and make it a cleaner and healthier place to live. You can also visit elderly people at a nursing home and spend time talking to them or playing games. You can read books to younger children at a local library or organize a toy drive for kids in need. These acts of kindness bring joy to others and make them feel loved and valued.

46. ENVIRONMENTAL AWARENESS

- You can help by reducing the amount of waste you produce. Instead of throwing things away, try to find ways to reuse them or recycle them if possible. For example, you can use both sides of a piece of paper for drawing or writing, or use old containers for storing things.

- Remember to turn off lights, fans, and other electronic devices when you're not using them. This helps save energy and reduces the amount of pollution that is released into the air.

- Be mindful of your water usage. Turn off the tap while brushing your teeth and take shorter showers. Water is a precious resource, so it's important not to waste it.

- Trees and plants are essential for a healthy environment. They produce oxygen, provide a habitat for animals, and help to reduce pollution. You can plant trees or even have a small garden at home to learn about plants and their importance. Take the time to learn about different animals, plants, and ecosystems. Visit parks, nature reserves, or even watch documentaries to understand how different species depend on each other and how human actions can affect them.

47. LEARN HOW TO RECYCLE

- Different things can be recycled, like paper, plastic, glass, and metal. It's essential to know what can and cannot be recycled in your area.

- Have separate bins or bags for different types of recyclables. Label them so everyone knows which items go where. You can use different colors or symbols for each type, like blue for paper, green for glass, yellow for plastic, and so on.

- Before putting items in the recycling bin, make sure they are clean and dry. Rinse out bottles, cans, and jars to remove any food residue. Wet or dirty items can contaminate other recyclables.

- If you have cardboard boxes, it's best to flatten them so they take up less space in the recycling bin. Large boxes can be broken down into smaller pieces.

- Recycling is important, but it's even better to reduce the amount of waste we produce. Try to use less plastic, choose reusable items like cloth bags instead of single-use plastic bags, and donate things you no longer need instead of throwing them away.

48. HOW TO GARDEN

- Find a sunny area in your backyard or balcony where you can create your garden. Most plants need at least 6 hours of sunlight a day to grow well.

- Good soil is important for healthy plants. Clear the area of any weeds or rocks. Loosen the soil using a small shovel or a garden fork. You can add some compost or organic matter to make the soil rich in nutrients.

- Decide what you want to grow in your garden. You can start with easy-to-grow plants like herbs (such as basil or mint), vegetables (like tomatoes or lettuce), or flowers (like marigolds or sunflowers).

- Follow the instructions on the seed packets or the plant tags to know how deep and far apart to plant your seeds or young plants. Dig a small hole, place the seed or plant gently, cover it with soil, and pat it down lightly.

- Plants need water to grow, so make sure to water them regularly. Use a watering can or a hose with a gentle spray attachment to water your garden.

- Keep an eye out for any weeds that may grow in your garden. Weeds compete with your plants for nutrients and water, so it's important to remove them.

49. BASIC HOME REPAIRS

- When a light bulb in your home burns out, you can replace it easily. First, turn off the light switch and let the old bulb cool down if it was just on. Then, carefully unscrew the old bulb from the socket. Take a new bulb, making sure it's the right size and type for your fixture, and screw it into the socket until it's snug. Finally, switch on the light to see if it works.

- Fixing a loose screw – Identify the loose screw and determine the appropriate size of screwdriver needed. Insert the screwdriver into the screw head and turn it clockwise to tighten the screw. Ensure not to overtighten, as it could damage the object.

○ If your sink is draining slowly or getting clogged, you can try to fix it yourself. First, remove any visible debris, like hair or food particles, from the drain opening. Then, pour some baking soda followed by vinegar into the drain. The chemical reaction will help break up the clog. After a few minutes, flush the drain with hot water. If it's still clogged, you can use a plunger to create suction and dislodge the clog. Keep plunging until the water starts to drain properly.

50. FIXING A LEAKY FAUCET

1. Turn off the water supply to the faucet by closing the shut-off valves under the sink.

2. Remove the faucet handle by locating the screw or cap on top of the handle and unscrewing or prying it off.

3. Use an adjustable wrench to loosen and remove the valve stem or cartridge.

4. Take the old washers or seals to a hardware store to find replacements.

5. Install the new washers or seals and reassemble the faucet in reverse order.

6. Turn on the water supply and check for any leaks.

51. HOW TO LEARN TO RIDE A BIKE

Make sure you have a bike that fits you properly. Sit on the bike seat, and your feet should touch the ground comfortably when you're sitting straight. Always put on your safety gear before you start riding. This includes a helmet, knee pads, elbow pads, and closed-toe shoes.

Start by sitting on your bike with your feet on the ground. Practice balancing by lifting your feet slightly off the ground and trying to stay upright. You can do this while someone holds the bike for you or by using training wheels. Once you feel comfortable with balancing, it's time to practice pedaling. When you're riding, always look straight ahead instead of looking down at your feet or the ground.

Learn to steer your bike by gently turning the handlebars in the direction you want to go. Start with wide turns and gradually make them tighter as you gain confidence. It's important to know how to stop your bike safely. Practice using both brakes evenly to slow down and come to a stop. Remember to use your front brake more gently to avoid flipping over. Keep trying, and with each practice session, you'll get better and more confident. Have fun!

52. HOW TO SWIM

Begin by practicing in a pool or a beach where you can comfortably touch the bottom with your feet and always under the supervision of an adult. Floating is an important skill that will help you feel relaxed and buoyant in the water. Practice floating on your back by lying flat, extending your arms and legs, and keeping your face towards the sky. Kicking is a fundamental swimming technique. While holding onto the edge of the pool or using a kickboard for support, practice kicking your legs up and down in a steady motion. To move forward in the water, you'll need to coordinate your arm movements with your kicking. Start by practicing the arm motions while standing in the water or holding onto the edge of the pool. Reach your arm forward, pull it back through the water, and then repeat with the other arm. Once you're comfortable with kicking and arm movements separately, try putting them together.

Breathing is essential while swimming. Learn to take breaths without swallowing water by turning your head to the side when your face is out of the water. Breathe in quickly and then turn your head back to the water as you exhale. Breathe in through the mouth and breathe out through the nose. Keep practicing and have fun!

53. HEALTHY EATING HABITS

It's important to eat different types of foods from each food group. There are five main food groups: fruits, vegetables, grains, protein, and dairy (or alternatives). Each group provides different nutrients that our bodies need to stay healthy and strong. Eat a rainbow of fruits and vegetables! Drink plenty of water. Water is the healthiest drink and it helps your body function properly. Eat meals together as a family! Eating meals together as a family can be a lot of fun. It's a chance to talk and spend time together. It also helps us make healthier choices because we can learn from each other and enjoy a variety of foods.

Limit sugary and processed foods. Foods that are high in sugar and unhealthy fats are not good for our bodies when eaten in large amounts. These include things like candy, cookies, soda, and fast food. It's okay to have them once in a while as a treat, but it's important to eat them in moderation.

54. MAKING A SIMPLE MEAL PLAN

Usually, people have three main meals (breakfast, lunch, and dinner) and a few snacks in between. So, you can start by planning for these three main meals and add snacks if you like.

It's important to have a balanced diet that includes different types of foods. Include fruits, vegetables, whole grains, and proteins in your meal plan. This will ensure you get all the necessary nutrients. Think about the foods you enjoy eating. You can include them in your meal plan to make sure you have something you love every day. It's okay to have treats occasionally, but try to focus on nutritious options most of the time.

Once you have your meal plan, make a list of all the ingredients you'll need. Check your pantry and fridge to see what you already have and what you need to buy. This will help you shop efficiently and avoid forgetting anything.

55. HEALTHY SLEEP HABITS

1. Try to have a consistent sleep schedule by going to bed and waking up at the same time every day, even on weekends. This helps train your body to know when it's time to sleep.

2. Make sure your bedroom is a quiet, comfortable, and dark place to sleep. You can use curtains or blinds to block out any light that might keep you awake.

3. Avoid using electronic devices like phones, tablets, or TVs for at least an hour before bedtime. The blue light from screens can trick your brain into thinking it's daytime, making it harder for you to fall asleep.

4. Before going to sleep, do something calming and relaxing. You can read a book, listen to soft music, or take a warm bath. This helps your body and mind relax and get ready for sleep.

5. Avoid drinks with caffeine, like soda or chocolate, especially close to bedtime.

6. Engage in physical activities and play during the day. It helps to tire out your body, making it easier for you to fall asleep at night.

7. Pay attention to how your body feels. If you're feeling tired, listen to your body's signals and go to bed. It's important to give your body the rest it needs.

56. EFFECTIVE NOTE-TAKING

- Start by using a notebook or sheets of paper dedicated to note-taking. Write the date and title of the topic you're studying at the top of each page.

- Pay attention to what the teacher or speaker is saying, or read the text carefully. Try to understand the main ideas and important details.

- Instead of copying everything word for word, try to summarize the information in your own words. Use short sentences and bullet points to jot down the main ideas. Use abbreviations and symbols. For example, instead of writing "because," you can use "b/c," or instead of "and," you can use "&."

○ If you're reading a book or using a textbook, you can use a highlighter or underline important sentences or words. This way, when you review your notes later, the important parts will stand out.

○ If you're learning something that involves processes or visuals, like a science experiment or a map, draw simple diagrams or pictures to help you understand and remember the information.

○ As you take notes, leave some space between each idea or section. This way, you can add more information or extra explanations later when you review your notes or get more details about a topic.

57. ACTIVE READING STRATEGIES

Before you start reading, take a moment to look at the cover, title, and pictures in the book. While reading, ask yourself questions about the story or the information you're learning. If you don't understand something, ask yourself questions to figure it out or write them down to ask someone else later. Based on what you've read so far, try to make predictions about what might happen next in the story or what you might learn in a non-fiction book.

Imagine the scenes and characters in your mind as you read. Visualize what they might look like or how they are feeling. Relate what you're reading to your own experiences, other books you've read, or things happening in the world around you. Jot down important points or interesting facts as you read. This can be done on a separate piece of paper or by underlining or highlighting key ideas in the book. After finishing a section or a chapter, take a moment to summarize what you've read in your own words. Try to capture the main idea or the most important points. Talk about what you're reading with someone else, like a friend, sibling, or parent.

58. TAKING CARE OF PERSONAL BELONGINGS

Keep your things clean and organized. Put your toys back in their proper places after playing with them, hang your clothes neatly, and keep your books on a shelf or a designated spot. This way, you can easily find them when you need them and prevent them from getting lost or damaged.

Be gentle when you use or play with your belongings. Avoid throwing or tossing them around, as it can lead to breakage or damage. Treat your things with respect and care, just like you would want others to treat your belongings. Follow the instructions and guidelines for using your belongings. If you have a new toy or gadget, read the manual or ask an adult for help to understand how to use it correctly. Using things the right way helps prevent accidents and keeps them working well. If you lend your belongings to friends or siblings, make sure they also understand how to take care of them. Talk to them about the importance of being responsible and gentle with your things. It's okay to share, but it's also important to set boundaries and make sure your belongings are treated with care.

59. PRACTICE SELF-REFLECTION

When we practice self-reflection, we can ask ourselves questions like:

1. How did I feel about what happened?
2. What did I do well?
3. What could I have done better?
4. How did my actions affect others?
5. What can I learn from this experience?

Self-reflection helps us become more aware of our strengths and weaknesses. It also helps us understand how our actions impact others and how we can make better choices in the future. Self-reflection can be done through writing in a journal, talking with a trusted adult or friend, or simply thinking quietly by ourselves. It's a great way to understand ourselves better and become the best version of ourselves. Remember, self-reflection is a skill that takes practice, just like learning to ride a bike or play a musical instrument. The more we practice self-reflection, the better we become at understanding ourselves and making positive choices.

60. PRACTICE SELF-CARE

- Getting enough sleep is important for your body and mind. It helps you have energy and be ready for the day ahead. Make sure you have a regular bedtime and try to get around 8-10 hours of sleep each night.

- Physical activity is not only good for your body but also for your mind. Go outside and play games, ride a bike, or simply run around. It's fun and keeps you active and healthy.

- Sometimes you might feel overwhelmed or tired, so it's important to take breaks. You can read a book, draw or color, or even just sit quietly and relax.

- It's important to do things that make you happy. Whether it's playing with your favorite toys, listening to music, or dancing, make time for activities you love. It helps you feel good and brings a smile to your face.

- If you're feeling sad, angry, or worried, it can help to talk to someone you trust. It could be a parent, a friend, or a teacher. Sharing your feelings with someone who cares about you can make you feel better and supported.

61. PRACTICE POSITIVE SELF-TALK

Start paying attention to the thoughts that pop into your head. Notice if they are positive or negative. Negative thoughts can make you feel sad or not confident, but positive thoughts can make you feel happy and strong. If you catch yourself thinking something negative like, "I can't do this," try replacing it with a positive thought like, "I can do my best, and I'll give it a try." This way, you're changing the negative thought into a positive one.

Use positive words when talking to yourself. Instead of saying, "I'm not good at this," say, "I'm learning, and I'll get better with practice." Positive words can boost your confidence and help you believe in yourself. Be your own cheerleader! Imagine you're giving yourself a pep talk. Say kind and motivating things to yourself, like, "I'm capable, I'm brave, and I can handle anything that comes my way." It's like giving yourself a high-five! Spend time with people who lift you up and make you feel good about yourself!

62. HOW TO IMPROVE SELF-ESTEEM

- Everyone has things they are good at. It could be playing a musical instrument, drawing, sports, or being a good friend. Focus on your strengths and celebrate them. Remember, you are unique and special in your own way.

- Think about what you would like to achieve, whether it's doing well in school, learning a new skill, or being kind to others. Set small, achievable goals for yourself and work towards them. When you accomplish your goals, it will boost your confidence and make you feel proud.

- Taking care of yourself is important for building self-esteem. Make sure you get enough sleep, eat healthy foods, and exercise regularly.

- Instead of saying negative things like "I'm not good enough" or "I can't do it," replace them with positive thoughts. Tell yourself, "I am capable," "I am smart," or "I can do anything I set my mind to."

- Remember that making mistakes is a normal part of learning and growing. When you make a mistake, don't be too hard on yourself. Instead, see it as an opportunity to learn and improve. Celebrate the effort you put into trying, and use it as a stepping stone for future success.

63. HOW TO PRACTICE SELF-MOTIVATION

Start by setting clear goals for yourself. These can be big or small, like finishing a school project, learning a new skill, or even getting better at a sport. When you have goals in mind, it gives you something to work towards and helps you stay motivated. Remember that you are capable of great things!

Sometimes, big goals can feel overwhelming. To make it easier, break your goal into smaller, more manageable tasks. When you accomplish each task, it will give you a sense of accomplishment and keep you motivated to keep going! Maintaining a positive mindset is crucial for self-motivation. Focus on the things you can do rather than the things you can't. If you encounter obstacles or setbacks, see them as opportunities to learn and grow, rather than as reasons to give up. Look for things that inspire you and keep you motivated. It could be reading books or stories about people who have achieved their goals, listening to motivational songs or speeches, or even talking to someone you admire.

64. RESPECTING DIVERSITY

Imagine if we all looked the same, thought the same, and liked the same things. Life would be pretty boring, right? Diversity makes our world colorful and interesting. It's like a beautiful garden with different types of flowers, each with its own shape, color, and fragrance. In the same way, people come in different shapes, sizes, and colors, and that's something to celebrate!

Respecting diversity means accepting that people can have different beliefs, traditions, and ways of doing things. It means being open to learning from others and understanding that just because something is different doesn't mean it's wrong. Treat others the way we want to be treated. Include everyone in our games, activities, and conversations. Be a friend to someone who might feel left out. If we see someone being treated unfairly because of their differences, we should speak up and support them. Discrimination is when someone is treated badly because of who they are, and it's not right. We can be allies and friends to those who need support. Instead of making fun of someone who is different, let's celebrate their uniqueness!

65. ACCEPTING CONSTRUCTIVE FEEDBACK

When someone gives you feedback, like a teacher, coach, or friend, listen carefully to what they are saying. Pay attention to their words and try to understand their perspective. Sometimes, feedback might feel a little bit hard to hear, but it's important to stay calm and not get defensive. Remember that the person giving feedback wants to help you improve.

If you don't understand something or need more information, it's okay to ask questions. This shows that you are interested in learning and growing. After you receive feedback, take some time to think about it. Consider the suggestions and think about how you can apply them to improve your skills or work. Once you've reflected on the feedback, try to put it into action. Use the feedback to make positive changes and work towards improving yourself.

66. GIVING CONSTRUCTIVE FEEDBACK

When giving feedback to someone else, it's important to be kind and respectful. Remember that the goal is to help the person improve, not to criticize or hurt their feelings. Instead of general statements like "You're not good at this," try to be specific and mention what they did well and what they can improve on. For example, say, "You did a great job on your drawing, but you could try adding more details."

Use "I" statements: Instead of saying, "You did this wrong," try using "I" statements to express how you feel. For example, say, "I think it would be even better if you tried this instead." Along with pointing out areas for improvement, offer suggestions on how the person can get better. Provide examples or demonstrate the steps they can take to improve their skills. Always remember to encourage and support the person you're giving feedback to. Let them know that you believe in their abilities and that you're there to help them grow.

67. DEVELOPING A GROWTH MINDSET

- Instead of avoiding difficult tasks, try to see them as opportunities to learn and grow. Remember that it's okay to make mistakes because they help you learn and improve.

- If you can't do something right away, don't worry! The word "yet" is important because it means that you haven't mastered it "yet." Keep practicing and learning, and you will get better over time. For example, if you say, "I can't ride a bike," try adding "yet" to it, and it becomes, "I can't ride a bike yet, but I'm working on it!"

- Feedback is valuable because it helps you understand how you can improve. When someone gives you feedback, listen carefully and consider it as a helpful suggestion, rather than as criticism.

- Look up to people who have achieved great things in the areas you're interested in. Understand that they didn't become experts overnight. They worked hard, made mistakes, and kept learning. Use their stories as motivation and proof that you can achieve your goals too.

- Don't give up easily when faced with difficulties or setbacks. Remember that progress takes time and effort. Stay determined, keep practicing, and believe in yourself.

68. MIND MAPPING

- To start a mind map, you'll need a blank sheet of paper and some colorful markers or crayons. In the center of the paper, draw a big circle or square, and write down the main topic or idea you want to explore.

- Next, think of all the different things related to your main topic. These are like branches that come out from the center of your map. For example, if your main topic is "animals," you can draw lines from the center and write down different types of animals, like cats, dogs, birds, and elephants.

- From each of those branches, you can create more branches for more specific ideas or details. For example, from the "dogs" branch, you can draw lines and write down different breeds of dogs.

- The great thing about mind mapping is that you can be as creative as you want. You can use different colors, draw pictures, and add doodles to make it more fun and engaging.

- Mind maps are helpful because they show the connections between different pieces of information. They help you see the big picture and remember things better. Plus, they make learning and organizing ideas more exciting!

69. UNDERSTANDING AND PRACTICING CONSENT

Everyone has personal boundaries, which are like invisible lines around our bodies and personal space. These boundaries define what feels comfortable or uncomfortable for each person. It's essential to understand and respect our own boundaries and those of others. When we want to do something that involves someone else, it's important to ask for their permission first. This could be as simple as asking if we can borrow their toy or play with them.

Consent involves both giving and receiving. If someone asks for our permission, we have the right to say "yes" or "no" based on how we feel. Similarly, if we ask someone for permission, we must listen to their answer and respect their decision, whether it's a "yes" or a "no." It's crucial to communicate clearly when it comes to consent. We should express our feelings and intentions honestly and respectfully. If we feel uncomfortable or unsure about something, we can say "no" or ask for more information. Consent can change at any time. Even if you initially gave permission for something, you have the right to change your mind and say "no" if you become uncomfortable or feel differently later on.

70. CULTURAL SENSITIVITY AND AWARENESS

Cultural sensitivity means being aware and respectful of the differences and similarities between people's cultures. It's like having a special kind of superpower that allows us to understand and appreciate how people from different parts of the world live, think and express themselves. Imagine if all the people in the world wore the same clothes, ate the same food, and celebrated the same holidays. It might be a little boring, right? That's because our world is filled with countless cultures, each one unique and beautiful in its own way!

When we're culturally sensitive, we try to put ourselves in other people's shoes and see the world from their perspective. We understand that people may have different beliefs, traditions, and ways of doing things. For example, some people may pray to different gods, eat different foods, or wear different types of clothing. And that's okay! Cultural sensitivity helps us embrace these differences and learn from them.

Being culturally aware also means being curious and open-minded. It's like having an adventurous spirit that loves exploring new things. We can learn about different cultures by reading books, watching movies, listening to music, and talking to people from different backgrounds.

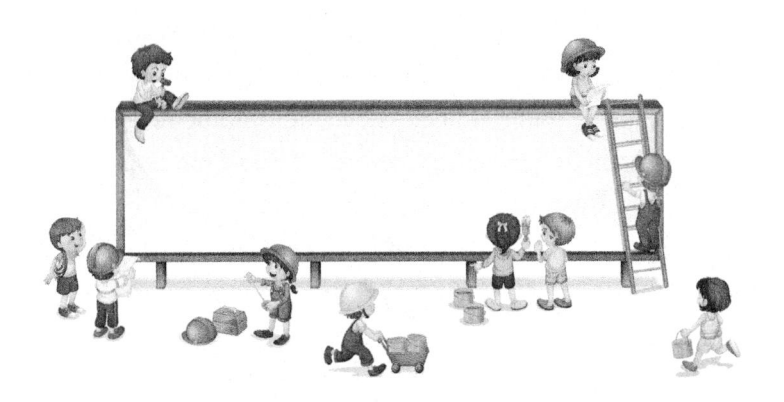

71. TEAM BUILDING ACTIVITIES

Human Knot – In this activity, you and your friends stand in a circle and each person extends their hand to grab someone else's hand across the circle. Once everyone's hands are connected, the challenge is to untangle the "human knot" without letting go of each other's hands.

Group Juggle – You and your friends stand in a circle and start with one ball. You pass the ball to someone else in the circle while saying the person's name. After a while, introduce more balls into the game, making it more challenging for the kids to keep track of the balls and pass them accurately.

Trust Fall – In this activity, you and your friends stand in a circle and take turns falling backward, trusting their teammates to catch them. This helps build trust and cooperation within the team!

Puzzle Solving – You and your friends can work together to solve puzzles or riddles as a team. This activity encourages problem-solving skills, communication, and the ability to work together towards a common goal!

72. HAVING A POSITIVE BODY IMAGE

Our bodies come in all shapes, sizes, and colors. It's important to remember that there is no "perfect" body. Each person is different, and that's what makes us special and beautiful. Instead of worrying about what you don't like about your body, try to focus on the things you do like. Maybe you have nice hair, strong legs, or a beautiful smile. Celebrate those things and be proud of them.

Remember that being healthy is more important than how you look. Take care of your body by eating nutritious foods, staying active, and getting enough rest. When you take care of yourself, you'll feel good on the inside, and that will reflect on the outside too.

Sometimes, we see pictures in magazines, on TV, or on social media that show people who look very different from us. It's important to remember that these images are often edited and don't show the real person. Instead of comparing yourself to those images, focus on being the best version of yourself. Treat yourself with kindness and respect. Instead of criticizing yourself or being too hard on yourself, practice self-love and self-acceptance!

73. BASIC STRETCHING ROUTINES

Warm-up – Before starting any stretching routine, it's essential to warm up the body. You can jog in place, do jumping jacks, or dance for a few minutes to get your muscles warm and ready.

Neck stretches – Slowly tilt the head forward, trying to touch the chin to the chest. Hold for a few seconds and then return to the starting position. Tilt the head to the right, bringing the right ear towards the right shoulder. Hold for a few seconds and repeat on the left side. Gently turn the head to the right, looking over the shoulder. Hold for a few seconds and repeat on the left side.

Arm and shoulder stretch – Extend the right arm straight in front and use the left hand to gently pull the fingers towards the body until a stretch is felt in the back of the arm. Hold for a few seconds and switch arms. Reach both arms overhead, interlace the fingers, and push the palms up towards the ceiling, stretching the shoulders.

Leg stretches – Sit on the floor with legs straight out in front. Slowly reach towards the toes, trying to touch them. Hold the stretch for a few seconds and release. Bend one knee and hug it towards the chest. Hold for a few seconds and repeat with the other leg.

Back stretches – Stand with feet shoulder-width apart. Slowly bend forward, reaching towards the toes or as far as comfortable. Hold for a few seconds and slowly come back up.

Cool-down – After completing the stretching routine, it's important to cool down the body. You can do light walking or slow jogging in place for a few minutes to gradually bring the heart rate down.

74. HOW TO MEDITATE

- Look for a calm spot where you can sit or lie down without distractions. It could be your bedroom, a cozy corner, or even outside in nature.

- Sit cross-legged on a cushion, or if you prefer, you can lie down on your back. Make sure your body feels relaxed and at ease.

- Gently close your eyes, which helps to shut out visual distractions and allows you to focus inward.

- Take a slow, deep breath through your nose, feeling your belly expand. Then exhale slowly through your mouth, letting go of any tension or worries.

- Pay attention to your breath as it goes in and out. You can even imagine your breath as a colorful ball of light moving in and out of your body.

- As you meditate, thoughts may pop into your mind. That's okay! Just acknowledge them without judgment and gently let them go. Imagine your thoughts as passing clouds in the sky, coming and going without holding onto them. Keep your attention on your breath.

- When you're ready to finish, take a deep breath in, slowly open your eyes, and take a moment to notice how you feel. You might feel more relaxed, calm, or even energized!

75. MEMORIZATION TECHNIQUES

- You can say the information out loud, write it down multiple times, or create a catchy song or rhyme to help you remember.

- Create vivid mental images to associate with the information you want to remember. For example, if you're trying to remember a list of fruits, imagine yourself holding each fruit and taking a bite. The more detailed and imaginative the images, the better.

- Create a word or phrase using the first letter of each item you want to remember. For example, to remember the order of the planets, you can use the mnemonic "My Very Eager Mother Just Served Us Nachos" (Mercury, Venus, Earth, Mars, Jupiter, Saturn, Uranus, Neptune).

- Write questions or information on small index cards. Put the question on one side and the answer on the other. Test yourself by flipping through the flashcards and trying to recall the answers. You can also make it a game by challenging a friend or family member to quiz you.

- Create a story or narrative that incorporates the information you want to remember. Our brains are wired to remember stories, so this technique can be quite effective. Make the story interesting, funny, or imaginative to make it more memorable.

76. HOW TO BE CREATIVITY

1. Let your imagination run wild! Think about different scenarios, make up stories, or create imaginary worlds. You can pretend to be a superhero, an astronaut, or a magical creature. This helps your creativity soar.

2. Grab some paper and crayons, and start doodling. Draw whatever comes to your mind, whether it's a funny character, a beautiful landscape, or a wacky invention. Don't worry about making it perfect. Just have fun and let your hand guide the way.

3. Explore various art forms like painting, sculpture, collage, or even origami. Experiment with different materials and techniques. You can use clay, paper, fabric, or recycled items to create unique artwork.

4. Words are like building blocks for creativity. Play word games, write silly poems or stories, or even make up your own secret language.

5. Challenge yourself to think differently. Ask questions like "What if?" or "Why not?" This can help you come up with creative solutions to problems or see things from new perspectives.

6. Spend time outdoors and observe the beauty of nature. Collect leaves, flowers, or interesting rocks. Use them to create nature-inspired crafts or artwork. Nature is a great source of inspiration for creative ideas.

77. THINKING OUTSIDE THE BOX

"Thinking outside the box" means being creative and finding new and different ways to solve problems or think about things.

Curiosity is the key to thinking outside the box. Ask lots of questions and explore different possibilities. Don't be afraid to wonder and imagine things that may seem unusual or different. Imagine that there are no limits or rules. Let your mind wander and think of wild and crazy ideas. Imagine what things could be like if they were different.

Try to see things from different points of view. Put yourself in other people's shoes and think about how they might approach a problem. Talk to others and share your thoughts and ideas. When you collaborate with others, you can combine your different perspectives and come up with even more creative solutions. Sometimes, it's helpful to challenge the rules and conventions. Think about why things are done a certain way and consider if there might be a better or different way to do them!

78. INNOVATIVE THINKING AND DOING

Innovative thinkers are always curious. They ask questions, explore new topics, and seek to understand how things work. Curiosity helps you discover new ideas and think outside the box. Innovative thinking involves being open-minded and receptive to different perspectives. Sometimes, the best ideas come from combining different thoughts and approaches. So, listen to others, respect their opinions, and be willing to consider new ideas.

Innovation often arises from identifying problems and finding creative solutions. When faced with a challenge, think about different ways to approach it. Don't be afraid to take risks or make mistakes; they can lead to valuable insights and discoveries. Innovative thinking is not just about having ideas; it's also about taking action to make them a reality. Once you have a great idea, think about how you can bring it to life. Start small, take one step at a time, and don't be afraid to ask for help along the way.

79. MAKING AND KEEPING APPOINTMENTS

When we want to meet someone or have a specific event or activity, we make an appointment. This means we decide on a date, time, and place to meet or do that particular thing. For example, if you want to have a playdate with your friend, you can ask your parent or guardian to help you set a date and time when you both can get together.

Once you've made an appointment, it's essential to keep it. Keeping an appointment means showing up at the agreed-upon time and place. It shows respect for the other person's time and ensures that everyone can make the most out of the planned activity. So, if you have a playdate at 3:00 PM, make sure you arrive on time so that you and your friend can enjoy your time together.

To help remember your appointments, it's a good idea to use a calendar or planner. Making and keeping appointments requires responsibility. It means taking the commitment seriously and doing your best to follow through. If you can't make an appointment or if something comes up that prevents you from attending, it's important to let the other person know in advance.

80. TAKING CARE OF A PET

1. Pets need to eat just like we do. Find out what kind of food your pet needs and how much to give them. Follow the instructions on the pet food packaging. Make sure to feed your pet at regular times every day and provide them with fresh water.

2. Pets need exercise to stay healthy and happy. Dogs, for example, love going for walks and playing fetch. Cats enjoy playing with toys and climbing on scratching posts. Find out what activities your pet enjoys and make time to play with them every day.

3. Just like humans, pets need to stay clean. Dogs and cats may need regular brushing to keep their fur neat and free from tangles. Some pets, like birds or reptiles, have specific needs for keeping their feathers or scales clean. Ask a grown-up to help you learn how to groom your pet properly.

4. It's important to keep your pet safe. Make sure your pet has a comfortable and secure place to sleep. Keep dangerous things out of their reach, like chemicals or small objects they might swallow. If you have a dog, always keep them on a leash when you go outside.

81. BASIC SELF-DEFENSE TECHNIQUES

- The first step in self-defense is being aware of your surroundings. Pay attention to what's happening around you and try to avoid potentially dangerous situations.

- Your voice can be a powerful tool. If someone you don't know approaches you and makes you feel uncomfortable or threatened, use a loud and firm voice to say "NO!" or "STOP!"

- Running away is often the best option in many situations. If someone is chasing you or trying to harm you, try to create distance and run to a safe place, such as a trusted adult, a store, or a crowded area.

- If you cannot escape and you need to defend yourself physically, aim for the person's weak points. Learning basic blocking techniques can help protect yourself. Practice using your hands and arms to block strikes directed toward you. Your legs are strong and can help you defend yourself. If someone is too close to you, use your legs to kick the person away from you. Aim for their legs, stomach, or groin area.

- It's important to have a network of trustworthy adults you can turn to if you ever feel unsafe or need help. This can include parents, teachers, coaches, or other responsible adults who can support and protect you.

82. RESPONSIBLE SOCIAL MEDIA USE

It's important to protect your personal information online. Never share your full name, address, phone number, or any other personal details with strangers on social media. Be cautious about what you post online, as once it's out there, it can be difficult to remove. Before sharing something on social media, ask yourself if it's something you would be comfortable with others seeing. Remember that once you post something, it can be shared or saved by others, even if you delete it later. Be mindful of the impact your posts might have on others.

Treat others on social media with kindness and respect, just like you would in real life. Avoid engaging in online arguments or bullying. Social media can be fun and entertaining, but it's important to find a balance. Spending too much time on social media can take away from other important things in your life, like spending time with friends and family, doing hobbies, or studying. Set limits on how much time you spend on social media each day. Not everything you see on social media is true. Before believing or sharing information, make sure it comes from a reliable source. Look for information from trusted news organizations or verified accounts.

83. BASIC COMPONENTS OF COMPUTER HARDWARE

- **The motherboard** is like the "brain" of the computer. It's a big circuit board that connects all the other components together. It has slots where you can attach things like the processor, memory, and other devices.

- **The processor**, also known as the central processing unit (CPU), is like the computer's brain. It does all the thinking and calculations. It's responsible for running programs and making the computer work.

- **Memory, or RAM (Random Access Memory)**, is like the computer's short-term memory. When you open a program or a file, it gets loaded into memory so that the processor can access it quickly. The more memory a computer has, the faster it can work.

- **The hard drive** is like the computer's long-term memory. It's where all your files, like documents, pictures, and videos, are stored even when the computer is turned off. Hard drives can store a lot of data, but they are slower than memory.

- **A graphics card** is a special component that helps your computer display images and videos on the screen. It's especially important if you play games or work with graphics-intensive programs like video editing or 3D modeling.

- **The monitor** is the screen you see and use to interact with the computer. It displays all the information from the computer so you can see what you're doing.

- **The keyboard and mouse** are the input devices for the computer. You use them to type, click, and interact with the computer. The keyboard is for typing, and the mouse is for moving the cursor on the screen.

84. BASIC COMPUTER LITERACY

- **The operating system** is like the computer's "boss." It's a special program that manages all the other programs and controls how the computer works. Examples of operating systems are Windows, macOS, and Linux.

- **Files** are like digital documents that you can create and store on your computer. **Folders** are like containers that help you organize your files. You can create folders and move files into them to keep things organized.

- **The internet** is like a huge network of connected computers around the world. You can use a web browser (like Chrome, Firefox, or Safari) to access websites and search for information. It's important to be cautious and only visit trusted websites.

- **Email** is a way to send electronic messages to people over the internet. You can create an email account and use it to send and receive messages, attach files, and communicate with others. It's important to be careful and not share personal information with strangers.

- **Word processing** is using a program like Microsoft Word or Google Docs to create and edit documents. You can type text, change fonts, add images, and format your document. It's a handy skill for writing assignments or creating stories.

85. BASIC CODING

Coding is like giving instructions to a computer so that it can do what we want it to do. Just like you can tell your friends how to play a game or follow a recipe, coding is a way to tell the computer what to do step by step. Coding helps us create computer programs, apps, websites, and even games! It's like a superpower that lets us bring our ideas to life and solve problems using technology!

Scratch is a fun and popular coding language designed for kids. It uses colorful blocks that you can drag and snap together to create your own interactive stories, animations, and games. You can make characters move, talk, and respond to your commands. Computational thinking is a problem-solving skill that helps us break down big problems into smaller steps that a computer can understand. It involves logical thinking, creativity, and organizing information in a clear way. It's like solving a puzzle or figuring out the steps to complete a task. When you start coding, you'll learn about things like loops, conditionals, and variables. Loops are like repeating actions, conditionals help make decisions based on certain conditions, and variables are like containers that hold information. Wow!

86. HOW TO NAVIGATE PUBLIC TRANSPORTATION

- First, decide where you want to go and find out which bus, train, or subway line will take you there. You can use maps, websites, or even smartphone apps to help you with this.

- Walk or get a ride to the nearest bus stop, train station, or subway station.

- When you board the bus or enter the train or subway station, you will need to pay your fare. There might be a ticket machine or a person at a booth where you can buy a ticket.

- Look for signs that show you which platform or track your train or bus will arrive on. If you're taking the subway, there will be different lines and directions marked on the walls.

- Pay attention to any announcements made over the loudspeaker. They will tell you when your train or bus is arriving, its destination, and any important information about delays or changes.

- Keep track of the names of the stops as you go along. If you're not sure, you can ask the driver, conductor, or fellow passengers.

- When you reach your stop, press the button on the bus or train to signal that you want to get off at the next stop.

87. BASIC CAR MAINTENANCE

Make sure the tires have enough air in them. You can use a tire pressure gauge to measure the air pressure and compare it to the recommended pressure mentioned in the car's manual. Also, look for any signs of damage or wear on the tires.

Oil is like blood for the car's engine. Regularly changing the oil helps to keep the engine running smoothly. You can ask an adult to show you how to check the oil level using the dipstick and how to add more oil if needed. There are other fluids in a car that need to be checked regularly, such as coolant, brake fluid, and windshield washer fluid. Ask an adult to show you where to find these reservoirs and how to check if the fluid levels are sufficient.

Washing your car not only makes it look nice but also helps to prevent rust. Get a bucket of soapy water and a sponge, and have fun cleaning the car's exterior. Don't forget to clean the windows too!

Wiper blades are important for clear visibility during rain or snow. If you notice that the wiper blades are streaking or not clearing the windshield properly, ask an adult to help you change them. The car's battery provides electricity to start the engine. Make sure the battery terminals are clean and free from corrosion. If you ever need to jump-start a car, always ask an adult for help.

88. BASIC CAR REPAIRS

Changing a Flat Tire

- When a tire goes flat, you need to replace it with a spare tire.
- Find a safe place to park your car and engage the parking brake.
- Use a jack to lift the car off the ground near the flat tire.
- Unscrew the lug nuts, remove the flat tire, and replace it with the spare tire.
- Tighten the lug nuts back on and lower the car to the ground.

Replacing a Headlight Bulb

- A headlight bulb may burn out over time and need replacement.
- Consult the car's manual to locate the headlight assembly.

- Unplug the electrical connector attached to the back of the headlight bulb.
- Remove the bulb by twisting it counterclockwise or releasing a spring clip, depending on the car model.
- Insert the new bulb, ensuring it's securely in place, and reconnect the electrical connector.

89. COPE WITH GETTING LOST

If you're with a group of people, like friends or family, make sure to stay close to them. The first thing to do when you realize you're lost is to take a deep breath and stay calm. Panicking won't help, and it can make it harder to think clearly and find your way. If you're in a familiar place and you feel safe, it's usually best to stay where you are. If you're in an unfamiliar area, look for a safe spot like a store, a restaurant, or a public place where there are other people around. Take a look around and try to spot any familiar landmarks or buildings. Look for things like tall buildings, unique signs, or recognizable features that you remember from the area. These can help you get your bearings and find your way back.

If you're lost in a public place or near other people, don't be afraid to ask for help. Look for a police officer, a security guard, a store employee, or a friendly-looking adult. Try to remember important information about yourself, like your name, your parents' names, and your phone number.

90. HOW TO PACK A SUITCASE

Pick a suitcase that is appropriate for the length of your trip. Make sure the suitcase is in good condition and has wheels, so it's easy to move around. Write down all the things you need to bring, such as clothes, toiletries, and any special items you might need for your trip. This will help you stay organized and not forget anything.

Spread out all the clothes you want to bring on your bed or a clean surface. Choose clothes that you can mix and match to create different outfits. Rolling your clothes instead of folding them can save space in your suitcase. Start with bigger items like pants and skirts, and roll them tightly. Then roll your shirts and t-shirts. This will help prevent wrinkles and make it easier to fit everything in.

Place your shoes on the bottom of the suitcase, near the wheels. Stuff your socks inside the shoes to save space. Then, put your toiletries like toothbrush, toothpaste, and shampoo in a separate bag or toiletry organizer. Make sure to put them in a secure bag to avoid any leaks. You can also pack other essentials like books, toys, or electronics in your suitcase. If you're traveling, remember to pack important documents like your passport, tickets, and any required identification.

91. HOW TO WRITE A PERSUASIVE ESSAY

Select a topic that you feel strongly about. Think about who you're writing for. Are you trying to convince your classmates, your teacher, or your family? Gather information about your topic. Look for facts, examples, and statistics that support your point of view. This will make your essay more convincing. You can use books, articles, or trusted websites for your research. Before you start writing, make an outline to organize your thoughts. Your essay should have an introduction, body paragraphs, and a conclusion.

Grab your reader's attention with a catchy opening sentence. Then, provide some background information about the topic and state your opinion clearly in a thesis statement. Each body paragraph should focus on one main idea or argument that supports your thesis statement. Start each paragraph with a topic sentence that introduces the main point. Then, provide evidence and examples to support your argument. You can also include counterarguments and refute them to strengthen your position. Summarize your main points and restate your thesis statement in a different way. End your essay with a strong closing sentence that leaves a lasting impression.

92. HOW TO PRIORITIZE TASKS

- Start by making a list of all the tasks you need to do. Write them down on a piece of paper or use a notebook or a digital device.

- Look at your list and think about which tasks are urgent and which tasks are important. Urgent tasks are the ones that need to be done right away, while important tasks are the ones that have a big impact or are meaningful to you.

- If any of your tasks have specific deadlines, mark them on your list. Think about the consequences of not completing certain tasks.

- Now that you have considered urgency, importance, deadlines, and consequences, it's time to assign priorities to your tasks. You can use numbers or symbols to indicate the priority level for each task. For example, you can use "1" for the most important and urgent tasks, "2" for the important but less urgent tasks, and so on.

- Begin working on the task with the highest priority. When you start working on a task, try to stay focused on it until it's finished. Avoid distractions like playing games or checking social media while you're working on your tasks.

93. FIRE SAFETY

- The best way to stay safe from fires is to prevent them from happening in the first place. Never play with matches, lighters, or any other fire-starting materials. Also, avoid touching or playing with things that get hot, such as stovetops, heaters, or electrical appliances.

- Make sure your home has smoke alarms installed on every floor, including near sleeping areas. Smoke alarms can detect smoke and give you an early warning if there is a fire. It's important to know the escape routes in your home. An escape route is the way you can get out of a building in case of a fire.

- If your clothes ever catch fire, remember to "Stop, Drop, and Roll." This means you should stop moving, drop to the ground, cover your face with your hands, and roll over and over to put out the flames.

- As soon as you notice a fire, you should yell for an adult and call the emergency number, such as 911, if it's available in your country. Tell them your name, address, and that there is a fire.

- If there is a fire, it's important to stay outside and not go back into the building.

94. HOW TO DEVELOP ADAPTABILITY SKILLS

Adopting a growth mindset is the foundation for developing adaptability skills. Embrace the belief that you can learn and grow from every experience, including setbacks and failures. View challenges as opportunities for growth and be open to new perspectives.

Instead of resisting or fearing change, actively seek it out. Take on new responsibilities, explore different roles, or volunteer for projects outside of your comfort zone. Understand your strengths, weaknesses, and areas for improvement. Reflect on how you respond to change and identify any resistance or rigidity in your thinking.

Engage with people from different backgrounds, industries, and cultures. This broadens your horizons and allows you to develop a more flexible and adaptable mindset. Stay curious and commit to lifelong learning. Be willing to adjust your plans and strategies as new information arises. Stay flexible in your approach and be open to alternative solutions. Surround yourself with a network of supportive individuals who can provide guidance and feedback. Seek mentors or role models who have demonstrated adaptability in their own lives and learn from their experiences!

95. PERSONAL HYGIENE

One of the most important things you can do to stay healthy is to wash your hands regularly. Use soap and warm water, and scrub your hands for at least 20 seconds. Taking a bath or shower helps keep your body clean. Use mild soap or body wash to lather up and wash your body from head to toe. Pay special attention to areas that sweat a lot, like your armpits and feet.

Keeping your teeth clean is essential for a healthy smile. Brush your teeth at least twice a day, in the morning and before bed. Use a soft-bristled toothbrush and toothpaste. Brush all sides of your teeth, your tongue, and your gums. Remember to replace your toothbrush every few months. Wash your hair regularly using a gentle shampoo and conditioner. Comb your hair to keep it neat and free of tangles. Keeping your nails clean helps prevent the spread of germs. Trim your nails regularly and keep them short.

96. HOW TO SHOW KINDNESS

Remember to say "please" and "thank you" when you talk to people. Using polite words shows that you respect and appreciate them. Then, sharing is a great way to show kindness. If you have something, like a toy or a snack, and someone else wants to play with it or have a bite, try to share it with them. And when it's someone else's turn to use or play with something, be patient and wait for your turn.

If you see someone who needs help, offer a hand. It could be helping a friend carry their backpack, holding the door for someone, or assisting a classmate with their schoolwork. Small acts of helpfulness can mean a lot to someone else. Sometimes, all someone needs is a listening ear. When a friend or family member is feeling sad or upset, be there for them. Listen to what they have to say and offer comforting words. Letting them know that you care and understand can make a big difference.

Remember that showing kindness to yourself is just as important! Take care of yourself by eating healthy food, getting enough sleep, and doing things you enjoy. When you are kind to yourself, you'll be better able to show kindness to others.

97. DO A GROCERY RUN

Before you go to the store, sit down with your parents or whoever is in charge and make a list of the things you need to buy. It's a good idea to bring your own bags to the store. Reusable bags are better for the environment because they can be used again and again. When it's time to go, hop in the car with your parent or guardian and drive to the grocery store. Grab a cart and make sure it's not wobbly. Look for the things on your list and put them in your cart.

As you put things in your cart, you can read the labels to make sure you're getting what you need. While you shop, you can also look at the prices of different items. Sometimes there are special offers or discounts. If you're not sure about something, you can always ask your parent or guardian for help. When you're done picking out everything on your list, it's time to go to the checkout area. There will be a counter with a cashier. After paying, you'll need to pack your groceries into the bags you brought with you.

98. PROPERLY USING AND CARING FOR TECHNOLOGY

It's important to handle technology devices, such as smartphones, tablets, and laptops, with care. Avoid dropping them or treating them roughly. They can be fragile and easily damaged, so it's best to be gentle when using and carrying them. Keep your devices clean by wiping them with a soft, lint-free cloth. Avoid using harsh chemicals or sprays, as they can damage the screens or casings. It's also a good idea to wash your hands before using touchscreens to keep them free from dirt and oils. To keep your technology safe, consider using protective cases, covers, or screen protectors. These accessories can help prevent scratches, cracks, or other damage.

Most technology devices need to be charged regularly. Follow the manufacturer's instructions for charging your device properly. Keep your devices up to date by installing software updates when they become available. These updates often include important security fixes and new features that can improve your device's performance. Ask an adult to help you with the update process if needed.

99. HOW TO HAVE NON-ELECTRONIC FUN

- Grab some paper, scissors, glue, and markers to create artwork, make paper airplanes, or build a cardboard fort. You can also try origami, creating jewelry, or painting.

- Gather your friends or family and play classic board games like Monopoly, Scrabble, or chess. Board games are a fantastic way to have fun, exercise your brain, and spend time together.

- Explore the fascinating worlds of books. Choose stories that interest you, whether they're about adventure, fantasy, or real-life heroes. Reading not only entertains you but also improves your vocabulary and imagination.

- Head outside and play games like tag, hide-and-seek, soccer, basketball, or catch. These activities help you stay active, improve coordination, and enjoy the fresh air.

- Go on a nature adventure! Visit a park, forest, or beach and observe plants, animals, and insects. You can also collect leaves, rocks, or seashells to create a nature journal or use them for art projects.

- Pack some delicious snacks and a blanket, and head to a nearby park for a picnic. Enjoy your food, play games, or simply relax in the great outdoors.

- Find something you're passionate about and turn it into a hobby. It could be drawing, playing a musical instrument, gardening, cooking, or even learning magic tricks.

100. HOW TO WATCH OVER A YOUNGER CHILD

Remember that you are in charge of keeping the younger child safe and making sure they are well taken care of. Take your role seriously and make sure to follow any instructions or rules given by parents or guardians. Pay close attention to the younger child at all times. Keep an eye on them and be aware of what they are doing. This means avoiding distractions like phones or other activities that might take your focus away from them. Make sure the area where you are watching the younger child is safe and childproofed.

Younger children love to play, so find fun activities to do together. You can play with toys, read books, build with blocks, or even have a pretend tea party. Engaging in play helps keep the younger child entertained and builds a bond between you. Make sure the younger child has regular meals and snacks throughout the day. Offer them healthy foods and encourage them to drink water to stay hydrated. If you're unsure about what they can eat, ask their parents or guardians for guidance. Depending on the age of the child, they may need help with things like going to the bathroom, getting dressed, or washing their hands. Be ready to assist them with these tasks as needed.

101. GETTING DRESSED AND READY

- When you wake up in the morning, it's time to start your day. Get out of bed and stretch your body to wake yourself up.

- Then, take a toothbrush and put some toothpaste on it. Brush your teeth gently in circular motions for about two minutes. Don't forget to brush the front, back, and chewing surfaces of your teeth.

- Next, it's time to wash your face. Wet your face with water and use a mild soap or face wash to clean your skin.

- Take a comb or a brush and gently comb your hair. Start from the top and work your way down.

- Choose your clothes for the day. You can pick out a shirt, pants or a skirt, and underwear. Make sure your clothes are clean and comfortable. Put them on one at a time.

- If you go to school or have any other activities, it's important to pack your backpack or bag. Put in your books, notebooks, pencils, and anything else you need for the day. Check your backpack to make sure you have everything you need.

- Before leaving the house, make sure you have everything you need. If it's a sunny day, you might need sunglasses or a hat. If it's cold outside, you might need a jacket or a sweater. Gather all your things and put them in your backpack or bag.
- Before you head out, say goodbye to your family members or caregivers.

Printed in Great Britain
by Amazon